Spirit Guides

A guide to connecting and communicating with your spirit guides!

Table of Contents

Introduction 1

Chapter 1: What Are Spirit Guides? 2

Chapter 2: Types of Spirit Guides 10

Chapter 3: Factors That Block Spirit Guides 19

Chapter 4: Communicating with Spirit Guides 24

Chapter 5: Staying Safe During Communication 29

Chapter 6: Frequently Asked Questions 35

Conclusion 40

Introduction

Thank you for taking the time to pick up this book on spirit guides!

This book covers the topic of spirit guides: what they are, how to safely communicate with them, and everything else you need to know about them.

Everyone has at least one spirit guide with them throughout their life. This guide aims to steer a person in the right direction, make the correct decisions throughout their life, and to help them achieve their goals and desires.

Learning to safely communicate with your spirit guide makes it much easier to ask them for guidance, to understand and interpret their advice, and to live a more fulfilled life. This book aims to fully educate you on these spirit guides and provide you with step by step strategies for safely and effectively establishing communication with your own guides!

Once again, thanks for choosing this book, I hope you find it to be helpful!

Chapter 1: What Are Spirit Guides?

Spirit guides are incorporeal beings, which are assigned to everyone before they are born. Spirit guides provide gentle guidance throughout a person's life, aiming to keep them from harm and move them in the right direction. Most people never communicate with their spirit guides or even know of their existence, but if they do appear, they do so in a manifestation that's comfortable to the person they are guiding.

Some guides are with you throughout your existence. Other guides will pop in from time to time and help you with certain goals that you're trying to attain. Such spirit guides exist at varying consciousness levels.

While spirit guides are essentially genderless, they may appear as male or female. They may even appear as animals or plants. In reality, spirit guides are just pure energy. They can be spirits who had physical incarnations in the past, or they may be spirits who have not ever existed in the physical world.

A person who a spirit guide is watching over, is known as a 'charge'.

You may be the only charge a spirit guide has, or they may be in a 'panel' of guides who have multiple charges. When it's time for the spirit guides to come to your aid, they attune to your energy and guide you towards your earthly purpose.

Know that spirit guides are never forceful, and they will never impose their teachings and guidance on you. They're simply gentle beings helping you on the right path.

Spirit guides can see your day-to-day activities. When you call on them, and they think it's time to intervene/guide, they have a few ways to let you know they're working for you:

Signs. Guides can help alert you to something that you should be aware of. Guides send synchronicities and signs, so you should be mindful of when they occur. This could be instances when events or things occur repeatedly. In this case, the spirit guides are trying to tell you something.

Gut Feelings. You may have a certain gut feeling when the guides are trying to tell you something. In such cases, it's best to follow your gut. Have you ever experienced a feeling that something bad was going to happen to you, but you weren't sure what it was? This may be your spirit guides warning you to be careful.

Intuition. Guides can send you images of intuition that seem like an inner voice. It's important that you pay attention to these feelings of intuition, as they can steer you away from danger, and help lead you to success.

Intuitive thoughts can appear randomly, but they usually provide vital information that you'll want to take notice of. A lot of people tune out intuitive thoughts, but they're highly valuable.

Sending Other People. Your spirit guide can confer with other spirit guides and they try to bring their charges to meet. You may randomly be thinking about someone who you haven't seen in a long time, and then, you see them in a café later in the day.

You may think it's a chance encounter, but it's actually not. Think of it not as a coincidence, but as the spirit guides setting you up.

Ways the Spirit Guides Can Help You

When you cultivate a relationship with your spirit guides, you will begin to receive spontaneous teachings from them, and experience shifts in perspective.

Your relationship with your guides is similar to your relationships with people close to you. Treat them like a family member or a true friend. If you and your guide don't know each other well and if you only communicate sporadically, your communication will likely be just surface-deep.

However, when you commit to thoroughly know your guide, you can quickly get nuggets of guidance and wisdom. You can 'hear' them in your thoughts, and you know that it's them. Spirit guides help you with subtle thought shifts. As time passes, they will help you overcome fears that keep you lonely, feeling small, and trapped.

How do the spirit guides help you in your day-to-day activities? How can you be in consistent communication with the spirit guides and still be able to complete your tasks? What are the benefits of constantly engaging with your spirit guides? The following is a list of the esoteric and practical ways that spirit guides can help you:

A Constant Presence

Spirit guides patiently wait for your requests to help you on particular issues. However, they're always present to direct and guide, and they do so in subtle ways.

For example, spirit guides may be trying to bring two people together to start a relationship. These two people did not exactly ask for each other specifically. They just unconsciously desired to meet a responsible and good partner. Thus, the guides worked to make these two individuals meet.

Spirit guides sense your unconscious desires and help to make them a reality. They can intervene and help to guide you in many situations such as in relationships, and business deals.

Expand Creativity

The combination of your spirit guides and your will is powerful. Such a relationship can help a person achieve great things in any domain.

Here's how spirit guides can help bolster creativity. In conversation together, either unconsciously or consciously, spirit guides are constantly feeding information to you. This is without exception.

If you actively try to be creative, you will be receptive to the information that your spirit guides are constantly sending you. This combination of your own desire to pursue a creative task, and their guidance in doing so, will deliver you great results.

Make the Things You Want Easier to Attain

Call on the spirit guides to help you attain what you what, and they'll clear a path for you to attain such things.

Many people never seek the guidance that they need, and as a result, never achieve what they desire.

If you are seeking a romantic partner, say a prayer to your spirit guides asking them to help you find a suitable person.

If you want a business deal to be successful, say a prayer to your spirit guides asking them to help you in such an endeavor.

Whatever it is that you desire, acknowledge your spirit guides, and actively ask them to help guide you to make the right decisions and meet the right people that will help you to achieve your goal.

Remind You of Patience

Patience is being able to witness and acknowledge divine timing, and to engage in creative endeavors for the time being. Your spirit guides can help you to cultivate patience.

At times, we can be impatient and allow our egos to control and wait incessantly. If you do this, what you seek may not be given to you. Instead, ask your spirit guides for a creative outlet, and ask them to help in strengthening your ability to be patient.

Let You Know When It's Time to Let Go

Spirit guides let you know when it's time to move on from a relationship, a job, a friendship, or a home, and you can either resist or accept this. Fear is normally the initial response to change. Fear slows advancement and limits growth as you live your life.

Things should not be unchanging and static. In your first two decades, you go through life constantly advancing and learning from one stage to another. As you enter your third decade, this shouldn't change. However, because there's no defined structure for it, since you're not in school anymore, people tend to become fearful of welcoming change and tend to avoid it at all costs.

Spirit guides can help you define the right course of action so you can do things with confidence and not fear.

Personal Lost and Found

Spirit guides can help you locate things that you've misplaced. For example, it may seem you have lost important notes for work. You've looked practically everywhere, yet you haven't found your notes.

In this instance, you may ask your spirit guides to help you. Close your eyes and ask your guides to be specific about where the notes are. The guides will then send you messages as to where your notes can be found.

Warn You in Times of Danger

When your spirit guides warn you in times of trouble or danger, they won't shout at you to get out of harm's way. The messages sent by guides are always subtle.

This could be a gut feeling to not walk down a certain street, or a sense that a person might not be trustworthy, despite how they seem outwardly. Pay close attention to these feelings and signs, as they are likely your spirit guides sending you a warning.

Assist You Even without Your Knowledge

If you think that you're not in communication with your spirit guide, or that perhaps your relationship is not evolving the way it should, you should understand that your spirit guide is still steering you in the right direction.

Knowing that your guide is always there helping you enables you to rest easy. The part of your mind that's connected to your spirit guide is always working, even if it's muddled temporarily by fear.

It's important to focus on the things you need and desire, as this will help you better receive messages from your spirit guide. If instead your mind is filled with fear and worry, it will become difficult to communicate clearly with your guide.

They'll Look Out for What You're Ready for

Spiritual growth can be overwhelming. It's as if your body's physical and electrical systems cannot handle your expansion in thought and creativity. Thus, spirit guides are careful not to deliver to you more than what you're ready for.

Spirit guides also take care in how they introduce you to joy, helping you to gradually open up so that the joy won't overwhelm and shock your system. Imagine a flower opening up to the sun, unfurling a petal one by one, slowly soaking up the sun before it becomes fully receptive and open. This is the same approach that spirit guides take when introducing you to new emotions and experiences.

As much as possible, the guides make it easy for you, especially when you are overwhelmed, or you feel frightened.

During times of creation and growth, take care of your physical body. Consume healthy food and drink a lot of water. It's also important for you to rest.

Perhaps, when you're communicating with the spirit guides, you may feel fatigued or start to yawn. Spiritual growth is highly demanding on the physical body, so pay close attention to how you feel.

Help You Get Ready for Challenging Conversations

If you're going to have a difficult conversation with somebody, pray to your spirit guides to guide the way before you engage in such a conversation.

For example, let's say you are entering into serious negotiations in a business deal. This conversation may involve a lot of disagreement, and perhaps even hostility.

By asking for guidance before even entering the conversation, your guides will help the conversation to run more smoothly, and from a place of respect. Spirit guides from both parties can change the energy before a conversation takes place, but you first will need to ask for their assistance.

Help in the Forgiveness Process

While forgiveness can be a noble ideal, it can be highly challenging in a world that is rife with hurt and suffering.

One thing that your spirit guide can do is walk alongside you as you get yourself out of fear and learn to be free to forgive. Forgiveness is a lengthy process.

When you seek true forgiveness, you mobilize a great support system. When you offer genuine forgiveness, you completely remove yourself from fear, and wipe the slate clean.

Detaching yourself from fear can happen only through forgiveness. When you seek to forgive, you're reaching your highest purpose. Ask your spirit guides for help in this difficult process, and you can be sure that they will assist you.

Open Your Spiritual Vision

Whenever you happen to be in a conflict situation, pray to your guides to help you see the situation from above. Instead of viewing from your ego, aim to view from your higher self. You should notice the difference. Your higher self will be non-judgmental.

As you collaborate with your spirit guides, you will start to see others and yourself the way your spirit guides do. You will start to visualize the light within and begin to detach yourself from outcomes and expectations. When you meet others, you will feel a desire to be kind rather than to be in control. You'll realize that drama is a waste of energy. You will begin to see the potential in yourself, and in others.

Chapter 2: Types of Spirit Guides

Spirit guides exist in your life to help you, and to push you in the right direction. They do not exist as an energy or entity that demands you to follow them. If your spirit guide is negatively influencing you, chances are that the entity is not actually your spirit guide. It may be a malicious spirit that's pretending to be your guide.

There are people who choose to break down and classify spirit guides by their purpose. Thus, spirit guides can be categorized as: gatekeepers, protectors, message bearers, teachers, healers, and guides to bring you joy.

Moreover, many people believe that their guides are also angels. This may or may not reverberate, depending on whether you accept that angels exist or not.

Here are some of the common spirit guides that are with us:

Ancestral Guides. An ancestral spirit guide claims a kinship with you, such as a relative who died when you were young. Even a long-dead ancestor can be a spirit guide.

Such entities are viewed as reincarnated guides. They are connected by blood to your family, or they can be spirits of people whom you loved while they were still alive. Some people refer to these ancestral guides as guardian angels.

Ascended Masters. Ascended masters are often worked with by people engaging in reiki or other energy work.

Ascended masters normally work with groups. That means if you have an ascended master as a spirit guide, you're not the only person being helped. These masters' main focus is to help humanity.

Teacher Guide or Common Spirit Guide. The conventional spirit guide is symbolic, representative, or archetypal of something else. An example would be you finding your guide to be in the form of a storyteller, warrior, or a wise man or woman.

These guides may introduce you to other archetypal guides on your journey. Based on your needs, they may help you solve problems.

Teacher guides are known to provide insight through meditation or dreams. As long as they're needed, they hang on. They move on after they have served their purpose.

Teacher guides also help in introducing you to people when you're ready for a necessary lesson. This type of guide can help you understand your soul contract, purpose, and overall lessons you need to learn in this life.

While going through challenges, teacher guides help you to understand the lesson and how it links to your higher purpose.

Call on your teacher guide when you find it hard to understand the lesson at hand or path in front of you. Teacher guides normally deliver their message by directing you to a person who will be the right teacher for you at a particular time. Teacher guides can also talk to you through synchronicities, dreams, and symbols.

Guardian Spirit Guides. The guardian spirit guides have protective roles and can intervene in your life in a physical way in order to offer protection. They can guide a car's movement, create protective energy around you, and can stop you from stepping into danger.

These guides can also talk to you through animal messengers. If you see an animal in an unusual place or an animal that you see repeatedly, it could be the spirit guide's way of reminding you to be strong and emulate that animal's qualities. The animal can remind you that you are protected physically.

Whenever you need protection, you can call on the guardian spirit guide. Just ask, and your guide will be there.

Gatekeeper Guides. These gatekeeper spirit guides help you navigate various Spirit World portals. They are gatekeepers between the different dimensions, and they exist to help you safely navigate through the Spirit World.

These guides can help you sharpen your intuition and can help you experience psychic activities like astral projection and lucid dreaming. These guides also protect you from penetrating too deep into the spirit world before you are ready.

Gatekeeper guides protect you from negative spirits and entities, and can help ease your transition into the afterlife.

Messenger Guides. These spirit guides come to you as you walk a new path or enter a new life chapter. They help to prepare you with necessary information and bring you messages through symbols and signs, which will help you make important decisions.

They also come into your life when you are about to make a major life choice or are at a crossroads. Messenger guides support you in your choices and also offer insights on the choices you make.

They communicate with you through dreams, synchronicities, symbols, or number patterns. They can also talk to you through clairvoyance or clairaudience. Intuitive readers or psychics often work with messenger guides to receive insights and messages on the person they're reading for.

To call these guides, just ask them to come to your life. Open a dialogue with them about your concerns and questions. Messenger guides always give answers as long as you open up to the messages' interpretation.

Helper or Healing Guides. These guides can heal emotional, physical, and energetic stresses and ailments. They offer you spiritual and emotional support in times of need.

These helper guides are present often in surgeries and in times of pain or sickness. They can be called on to help hasten the healing process. These spirit guides can also be called on during times of emotional trauma or if you're feeling negative or down.

These particular spirit guides work with people in the healing or medical profession and act often as a facilitator or mentor to healers or doctors as they work. If you are in such a noble profession, you may feel this entity guiding you.

Totems/Animals. As spirit guides, animals are well-known and have become popular over the years. This may be due in part to their accessibility in people's lives. Some ancient cultures, like the Chinese and the indigenous Americans, had animals to represent their lineages or tribes.

Nowadays, animals reflect and represent a person's own inner needs and yearnings. When animals were once used to represent groups, they now increasingly represent individuals.

In certain spiritual traditions, an individual can have an animal totem, which provides protection and teaching.

Trans-Species (Half-Beast/Half-Man). Spirit guides usually manifest as a white light. When they manifest as visual beings into your mind's eye, however, they can sometimes take the form of half-animal and half-man/half-woman.

Examples of these mixed species are fauns, centaurs, sphinxes, fairies, mermaids, and Minotaur beings. A lot of deities also manifest as spirit guides.

Some of these deities include Ganesha (Indian God with an elephant's head), Anubis (Egyptian god with a jackal's head), Ra (human body-falcon head), among others.

Gods and Goddesses. Since the beginning of time, gods and goddesses have been feared, worshipped, and written about. These entities span across every tradition, culture, religion, and in every part of the world.

The usual deities that serve as spirit guides include Apollo, Athena, Quan Yin Lugh, Lakshmi, Hathor, Kali, Horus, Selene, and The Green Man.

Plants. There are shamans who believe that the world and all things in it are comprised of living, vibrant energy. Plants are also believed to have energy. Ayahuasca (a psychoactive brew derived from plants growing in Peru) is one of the common ways to communicate with nature's spirits. The 'vine of the souls' (Banisteriopsis Caapi) is taken by individuals who want to feel guided into the realms of outer and inner existence. The same also holds true for other psychoactive plants.

Plants may be symbolic, like in Pagan rituals that associate plants with certain qualities, or experiential, wherein ingesting the plants stimulates physical, emotional, and mental expansion.

Spirit guides are just as diverse and varied as human beings are. During your lifetime, you are likely to have multiple spirit guides for various purposes.

Whether you want to connect with your spirit guide through singing, trance, meditation, simple observations, rituals, or psychoactive journeying, it's a comfort that your spirit guides are always there for you.

What the Spirit Guides Want to Tell You

Spirit guides are our teachers in life. You can't go through life just armed with what you learned in school. It's imperative that you continue to learn throughout your life.

When you're in touch with your spirit guides, you'll find out that they want to impart tidbits of wisdom to you. Tap into your spiritual side and allow your guides to teach you valuable lessons.

Be Fully Divine and Fully Human

You can find meaning in even the most mundane things with your spirit guides' wisdom. Since time immemorial, human beings have had a deep association with the physical environment and the land around them.

For their existence, humans rely on the sky, the earth, the heavens, animals, and plants. However, the bond with the environment is greatly suffering, as many of us are not aware of how the environment is vital to our survival.

One reason to be in constant communion with the spirit guides is to honor and remember the world around you. This may seem unusual as spirit guides are focused on the metaphysical; the unseen. However, the whole point of the guides' relationship with you is to help you grow in a spiritual sense and let you love the physical world better.

Spirit guides work with you so you can be more comfortable in your physical existence and in your own skin. At the same time, you understand that your existence does not define you. This may seem like a contradiction and a conundrum.

To be both human and divine, you need to become mindful. As you work with your guides, you will slow down and gradually become more aware of the environment that you live in.

This is to remind you that the physical world is a place of creativity and wonder. If you don't pay attention to the mountains, rivers, and trees, you'll miss much of the appeal that life on this planet has.

Whether you're aware of it or not, you're rooted to the land by your existence. From time to time, it's also important to replenish and nourish your relationship with the land, even if you live in an urban jungle where natural beauty is a rarity. You can admire the sky and the clouds, even if trees are not present. You can also be grateful for the water coming out of the faucet.

Why are such things important in your relationship with spirit guides? They bind you to your physicality and fill your cells up with memories of physical heritage. Spirit guides help to connect heaven with the earth. If you're not connected to the land, the guides' messages will not be able to properly reach their destination.

Be conscious of the environment and nature around you. Be thankful for the food you eat, and the water you drink. Take time to walk around in nature, and fully embrace the incredible environment that you are blessed to exist in.

Thoughts as Building Blocks

Your thoughts may seem random and fleeting. From a human viewpoint, thoughts can seem to be easily forgotten.

At the same time, thought is also concrete and elastic. Thought has a shape, an energy, an intention, and an effect. Part of the reason why spirit guides work with you is to help you mold those thoughts, to practice discipline, and to control what passes through your mind.

You can think of loving thoughts literally as the building blocks for anything that you can create and achieve in life. Loving thoughts provide that foundation. Thus, you can train your mind to cultivate such thoughts. Focus on loving thoughts, rather than thoughts of hatred, fear, or resentment. Ask for assistance in this endeavor from your spirit guides.

Live Life without Worry

In the world of the spirit guides, there's no worry. There's only knowledge that all is well. There's trust, and there's contentment and peace.

Spirit guides are secure, they're not defined by money, don't develop ailments, and are not limited by religious beliefs. For spirit guides, worry is a foreign concept, although they're aware how it affects us on the temporal plane.

Even while we're in a physical body, we experience what spirit guides experience.

This is what you can do. For five minutes, sit quietly and imagine that you're existing in a non-physical form, just like your spirit guides. This can be difficult as you start out. With practice, however, this activity becomes relatively effortless.

This is what you do often when you dream. You return to the non-physical and escape the physical. Thus, the limits of space and time don't apply in dreams. Things may also not make any sense.

As you daydream, the point is to achieve the non-physical. Feel what it's like to go anywhere without a body. Imagine how it is not to feel or dread illness. Experience what it is like is to know you don't have any money problems. Everything you need and want is already there.

Imagine that you're surrounded by people who love and care for you. Imagine you can soar, jump, fly, whiz around, and leap without limitations. Imagine not directing judgment, anger, or blame toward anyone, because there's no cause for anger as fear doesn't exist.

Do this imagination exercise daily. Let yourself fully feel the sensations and emotions of such things in your body and mind. You'll be triggering a portion of your mind's higher self.

With this activity, you'll be able to reduce worrying. As time passes, you'll be much less reactive to worry since your default is now a feeling that makes worrying impossible. The worry feeling will now be foreign to you, and the norm will now be that 'all is well.'

Do this activity each day. The ego may try to be a hindrance. Go against what the ego wants and do it, enjoy it.

You Are Creative

Many people manifest creativity, while others don't express their creativity freely. The truth is, everyone is creative. Hence, creativity is the intentional partnership between the spirit world and the temporal world brought into our world by our willingness to listen.

Creativity manifests in ways you may not be aware of. It is creativity if you love to spruce up your home. It's also creativity if you love to develop smartphone apps. Such things are more fun and easier if you work together with your spirit guides.

It's not that some people are creative, and others are not. It's that the ones who seem to be more creative are in tune with their spirit guides and the guidance they provide.

Everyone is the embodiment of creativity. Listen to the spirit guides about how to use that creativity. When you do, life flows happier and easier. Creativity may be considered problem solving. Problems, however, can be the result of one's own imaginings. You make a problem, and then come up with a solution.

Chapter 3: Factors That Block Spirit Guides

If you're struggling to communicate with your spirit guides, there may be a problem. There may be an underlying reason why you haven't felt their presence, and why your spirit guides' communication to you is blocked. Simple factors like the food you eat, or your attitude can affect your connection with them.

Below are common problems that many people, including you, are likely to encounter that can affect communication. In your life's journey, you may discover other factors that block communication with your spirit guide. Take the following factors as a starting point and look to your lifestyle and what's within your heart to determine what changes you may need to make.

Disorganization. You tend to attract the things that surround you. Is your home full of clutter? Is your room a mess? Your surroundings' state can reflect your heart. Decluttering your living space, and even using something like Feng shui to help you to decorate can be a huge help in improving your environment.

Your spirit guides are attracted to clear and clean environments. Make things easier for your guides and create the most welcoming, appealing atmosphere possible for them.

Inexperience. Like everything else, practice makes perfect; that includes communicating with your spirit guides. In this case, the best practice is not to overthink things.

While you should keep an open mind and heart, you should also learn to calm your mind. You can do this through daily meditation, keeping realistic expectations, and learning patience.

You may also increase your awareness by heightening your senses. Don't be always looking out for your spirit guides. Don't look for signs in everything you see. Instead, aim to be in the moment, and let the signs come to you.

Impatience. If you're anxiously waiting for, and wondering about your spirit guides' messages, the internal anxiety and turmoil that's building up within you could cause you to miss your guides' messages. Moreover, when you're in an anxious state, it's difficult to have faith in your guides.

Being patient also makes you trust your spirit guides and strengthens your bond with them.

Great miracles happen when you aren't looking for them. When you have a strong connection with your guide, you'll begin to understand that coincidences are often actually intentional guidance and messages from your spirit guides.

Expectations. Are you doing nothing and are just waiting for a giant sign to fall down and hit you on the head? Instead, try to focus on your connection with your spirit guides.

There's no way for you to know how exactly your guides will reach you. By setting high expectations and constantly waiting for them, you're limiting yourself and closing your channels of spiritual connection.

The way they reach out to you may be grand, or it may be subtle. At times, they may just be gentle whispers in your ears, mere feelings in your heart, or just fleeting visuals.

Chance upon the smaller signs and don't expect those big thunder-and-lightning events. Once you're in communication with your guides, you'll then realize your journey with the spirits and the little signs are what matters most.

Food. We are all energy wave clusters. As a human being, you choose to view yourself as a solid form via consensus reality. In fact, everything you drink and eat, and everything you put into and around your body affects your entire wellbeing's overall vibration. We are – after all – energy. Since food is energy, it in turn affects your energy.

Be mindful of the vibrations of the food you consume. When you consume food with a rapid and high vibration, you can hold a healthy, strong, joyful, and exuberant state.

Conversely, when you consume food with a lower, slower frequency, your vibrations are lowered, and you may not feel rejuvenated throughout the day.

You have your own signature vibration, as do the rest of us. Each piece of food you eat contributes to that vibration. Some of the lower-vibration food that you should limit or avoid includes:

- White flour and rice.
- Soda.
- Coffee.
- Sugar and other sweeteners.
- Alcohol.
- GMO (genetically-modified organisms) food and conventional food treated with pesticides and chemicals.
- Fish, meat, and poultry.
- Packaged, processed, canned, and fast food.
- Frozen food.

- Unhealthy oils like cottonseed, canola, vegetable oils, and margarine.

- Deep-fried food, cooked food, and microwaved food.

- Pasteurized yogurt, cheese, and cow's milk.

Drama. The chaos brought on by certain situations and relationships may be utterly distracting. When you're constantly trying to make others happy or you're always arguing with an acquaintance (a spouse, partner, friend, family member, or coworker), you're not likely to be happy yourself.

You're likely closed off, unfocused, and agitated. This may make it hard for you to commune with your spirit guides.

Let your guides help in clearing your heart. Get rid of the fear and negativity and replace it with positivity's loving, peaceful, energy. Also let your guides help to end any relationships that are more harmful than helpful, are slowing you down, and those that you have outgrown.

It's alright to let go of relationships that are draining you of valuable spiritual and emotional energy. It's still important to love the people around you, including family. Just choose those whom you want to reveal yourself to.

The more negative energy surrounding you, your friends or family included, the harder it will be for your guides to communicate with you.

Overanalyzing. Inflated egos can be one of the biggest hurdles when trying to communicate with your spirit guides. When the ego is telling you that it knows best, you need to drown it out for a while.

Have faith in your guides. Faith opens the space for the miracles your spirit guides want for you. While such miracles are not crazy, drastic, or earth-shattering each time, let those miracles flow effortlessly to you. Shut off the ego, and allow your spirit guides to take control because they truly know best.

Chapter 4: Communicating with Spirit Guides

There are so many ways to communicate with spirit guides, and they also communicate in unique ways. They communicate with you primarily through strong thoughts. Spirit guides deliver messages in a similar way that messages are sent through mediums (spirit interactors).

Spirit guides' connection with humans is gentle. The way they communicate with you is not always through mental insight or intuition. The best way to think about spirit guide connections is to consider them as concerned directional messages.

Your relationship with your spirit guide or guides is also unique. Like any relationship with a loved one here on earth, cultivate your relationship with your spirit guide with caring and nurture.

Your relationship with your spirit guide needs the same amount of time and commitment as any other important relationship in your life. The more attention and time you give to cultivating communication with your spirit guide, the stronger your relationship with your guide becomes.

There are several ways to contact your spirit guide. We'll discuss a few ways in this chapter. To begin, here is one of them:

Find a quiet area in your home or office and sit in a relaxed manner. This is needed to reach the meditative state wherein you and your guide will meet initially. However, do know that your guide has always been with you. You simply have not made communication with them yet.

At such a point, say a prayer inviting your guide to contact you. An example would be, 'Spirit guide, I invite you. I would like to have an open communication with you.'

Once you've invited the spirit guide, listen to your surroundings and trust your guide to be in contact with you. The important thing is to be patient. At first, communication may not be clear since this is a relationship that requires a good deal of vibrational energy. Don't try too hard and let the guidance and messages come to you naturally.

Spirit guides will sometimes tell you their names, though not always. In any case, the spirit guides are not usually particular about what they're called. If you must know their names, ask them while you meditate and trust the first name that you come across.

Simple Ways to Connect

You may have just one spirit guide, or you may have multiple. Guides exist in your life for a particular purpose. If you need to make a decision, there's a spirit guide for that. If you simply want to learn lessons in life, you can call on a teacher guide that may introduce you to someone who can help you on your journey.

You always have a spirit guide within you, waiting for you. All you need to do is to call it and it will have a message for you. Below are some ways you can effectively call and communicate with your guide.

Ask Clearly. Spirit guides can help you in many ways. They can help you find lost car keys or help you heal a broken heart. Other matters in your life that spirit guides can help you with is getting through challenges, meeting your future life partner, finding the courage to reach your potential, and helping you overcome the past and move forward.

For the spirit guides, no request is too small or too big, too broad or too specific. Since we are in a world where free will is respected, to let your spirit guides in, you must ask them first to come into your life.

Don't Lust for the Outcome. There are some who have tried to communicate with their spirit guides but had disappointing results. Many of them waited for long periods before finally being able to communicate with them.

Let go of any expectations about how the spirit guides should reveal themselves to you. Just remain open-minded and allow the guides to communicate with you in whatever way they see fit.

Do an Attunement Meditation. Your spirit guides are always with you. All you need to do is to connect with them. Tuning into a frequency of the same wavelength as them, however, is not always that easy.

Performing spirit guide attunements or meditation is an excellent way to initially connect with your guides.

Create a Guidance Box. Have a special box to help you communicate with your spirit guides. On a piece of paper, write down a specific thing that you need their help with, or write down a question for them to answer. Fold up the piece of paper and place it in a box. Keep an open mind and you may find the answers you seek.

Have a Sacred Space. Select a sacred space in your home. This is where you can connect with your spirit guides each day. It may be as simple as your bedside table, or a window ledge.

Set aside time each day to connect with your spirit guides. In order to cultivate your relationship with your guides, you must regularly invest time into it.

Write with Intuition. One way to connect with beings in the spiritual realm, including your spirit guides, is through intuitive writing. Begin by clearing a sacred space. Light a candle and sit down with two pens of different colors and your journal.

Write your first question with your first pen. Using the second colored pen, ask the spirit guides for an answer and let the answers flow from your intuitive hand and on to the page.

Call Your Team. If you're working on an important project, call the best spirit guides to help you in your endeavor. If you're writing a book, for example, recruit a spirit guide who has written poetry or books of their own. These guides may once have been living beings that have transcended into the beyond. If you're going through a hard time with your writing project, you may choose to call on a teacher spirit guide to help you.

Don't Micromanage Your Guides. Trust your guides to do the job for you. It's like in a conventional workplace. The best managers are the ones who are clear about the work and then trust that their teams can capably do the job.

Be clear on what you want your spirit guides to do. Let them guide you and then trust they can do the job well. Never doubt your spirit guides. Never micromanage them. Just trust in them, and you'll be amazed with the results.

Keep a Diary for Your Guides. Note down any visions, guidance, intuitive hunches, or dreams that you may receive. Connecting with your guides requires you to trust and notice the guidance as you receive it. When you write it down, you create a record of what messaged you receive, and you'll soon have a clear picture as to how your guides are helping you.

Sleep Well. Sleep is an excellent way to connect with your guides. As you go to bed, ask your spirit guides to come to you. When you wake up the following morning, take note of the messages that you received in your dreams.

Chapter 5: Staying Safe During Communication

It can be an exhilarating experience when you communicate with your spirit guide. You're excited with the thought of accessing a dimension that's magical and greater than the things you see on this earthly plane.

You can access the spirit world if you keep your mind and heart open. However, there may be darker forces at play, and it may not always be your spirit guide that's communicating with you.

Spirits can visit you even if there's no proper invitation, such as a departed loved one. A spirit will often visit through a certain space in your home. This is because they want to let you see something important, or they have a message of some sort for you.

Engaging in the spirit world is entering the unknown. Thus, you need to protect yourself with the right tools.

Be Protected. Before attempting to communicate with your spirit guides or the spirit realm, protect your space and your energy. Charge up your protective energy through meditation. Imagine a white light enveloping your entire being. You may also use protective crystals, an example of which is amethyst.

Set up a Sacred Space. Create a sacred space if you wish to get information from a spirit, or if you wish to talk to a departed loved one. Such a space must be clear and safe from distractions or clutter.

You may fill this space with plants, crystals, herbs, candles, or other items that make you feel good. Keep handy a paper and pen if you want to write down things.

Set Your Intentions. Once in the sacred space, set your communication intention. Be clear about the communication experience that you desire. Firmly state your intentions and set boundaries.

You can say:

'I want to connect with the spirit of (name here). I am protected and guided to hear the messages that (name of spirit) has for me. I ask the angels to protect me and help me receive any necessary messages.'

When dealing with the unknown, first feel out the energy. If you're uncertain, or if you feel a certain negativity, then stop.

If you want to communicate with spirit guides or other spirits, it doesn't help to be fearful or scared. If you have such feelings, stop until you can access the spirit realm with a clear and positive mind.

Be Open to Messages. When you have set your intention, talk to the spirit as if it's already in the space with you. Ask the spirit questions and wait to see if it will answer you back. When the spirits answer you back, you'll be feeling varying sensations.

You may feel tingles and bodily sensations, hear audible messages, or see sparks of light, or synchronistic signs. Be open to communication and write down anything you feel or see.

Tools that can help you receive spirit messages include pendulums and automatic writing. Pendulums are an excellent beginner's tool and are less intimidating than automatic writing.

During the communication process, you should understand that you won't likely get your answers immediately. Be gentle and patient and know that you'll find your answers when and if you're meant to. Keep an open mind. You may often receive or feel the answers, but may not realize them to be answers as they're not what were expected.

Close the Door. Once you're done asking your questions, announce you're done and 'close' the session. You may want to send off the spirit by thanking them for their messages and saying goodbye.

Thereafter, cleanse your aura and space with bells, sage, crystals, or incense. You should not miss this cleansing step. Even if you haven't established a connection, do the cleansing process and properly end the session.

If can be enlightening when you can properly communicate with spirits or your spirit guides. As long as you take precautionary steps and don't rush into anything, there's no reason why you cannot benefit from establishing contact with the other side. Just protect yourself and be grateful to the spirits that you communicate with.

Things to Avoid when Communicating with Spirits

While you need to protect yourself spiritually before your communication with the unknown and with your spirit guides, there are also things that you should avoid in order to establish and maintain a positive connection.

Avoid Drinking Alcohol or Taking Drugs When Communing with Spirits. Substances pave the way for another door to the spirit world, whether you want to talk to them or not.

If you drink alcohol or take other substances, you enable all kinds of energy to enter, especially the energies drawn to the low vibration linked to intoxication. Such spirits that may enter could be malicious or mischievous, and cause a great deal of trouble.

Avoid Communication when Unhappy, Imbalanced, or Feeling Negative. People tend to attract like energies. Thus, when you're negative or unhappy when trying to call on spirits, you attract similar energies as you.

Let your moods be frequencies, which are signals emitted at a certain vibration that – in turn – draw back to you entities and energies that exist at the same frequency.

If you're set to the frequency of love, you attract loving spirits and entities. Conversely, if your frequency is of negativity, you will draw in negative energies and spirits.

Avoid Contacting Spirits with Other People Who Are Unhappy, Imbalanced, or Negative. If you can't attract good spirits and energies if you feel negative, the same goes for people who are attracting spirits and energies with you.

If you're in a group, ensure that all of you have the energies of love and positivity. Anyone near you as you try to call on the spirits can either contaminate or contribute in the process, depending on their energetic disposition.

Avoid Communicating with Spirits When You're Exhausted or Fatigued. When you are physically tired, you're vulnerable and less in touch with your spiritual side.

When you're exhausted or fatigued, it's easier to misunderstand messages or misread energies. Thus, the process of calling the spirits can go wrong. Be well rested, physically and mentally, before calling on spirits.

Avoid Fear. If you're afraid to contact your spirit guides, don't do it. If you're a little bit afraid, but you are curious, don't call the spirits. Instead, read books and talk to people knowledgeable on the manner, so that they can help you become comfortable about the spirit-calling process.

When dealing with spirits, make sure you're healthy and positive. Drive out your fear, as continuing to be fearful may attract malicious entities that want to play on that fear.

Avoid Communicating with Spirits That Tell You to Listen Only to Them. Spirits wanting to make your life better will not impose their judgment on you. They will neither control you nor tell you what to do. Good, higher-level spirits present options, offer insight, and make suggestions.

These spirits want you to decide on the best choice for you. They will not be upset if you don't follow their advice. Don't work with an energy or spirit that seeks to control you or wants you to do tasks that don't feel right to you. This means that you're working with a spirit that's non-evolved.

Avoid Working with Non-Evolved or Unenlightened Spirits. Work with your spirit guides or high-level entities like angels. While your spirit guide is always with you, maybe you can chance upon a spirit that doesn't have your best interests at heart.

Avoid communicating with earthbound spirits as they're people who are dead. Whether dead or alive, people are limited by what they desire and know.

An earthbound spirit may know the same things as you, yet their intentions are different from yours. You may recognize a non-evolved or unenlightened spirit based on their vibration rate.

Love vibrates at a joyful, high, and delightful energy. On the other hand, non-evolved spirits vibrate at a negative, low, uncomfortable, and fearful energy. Know the difference between positive and negative energies and be mindful of them.

Chapter 6: Frequently Asked Questions

Here are some of the most common questions that people ask when first trying to communicate with their spirit guides:

Q. What do guides look like?

A. Not everyone knows what their guide looks like. They often manifest as pure energy. If you feel you see your guide, it's normally in your mind's eye instead of an actual manifestation.

Whenever you feel or 'see' them, their energy depends on what you want to accept. Your spirit guide wants you to be happy and relaxed. If you feel comfort when accepting their energy, your spirit guide will appear to you as energy.

However, if you worry about your guide manifesting as energy, your spirit guide may manifest in your mind's eye in human or animal form.

Q. Are spirit guides the same as guardian angels?

A. From birth, you have your assigned spirit guide. Your guide is concerned with you and its only thought is your wellbeing. Spirit guides are not the same as guardian angels.

Guardian angels are a bit further up in the spiritual hierarchy. Guardian angels look after groups of people. A guardian angels' job is more of an oversight of multiple people; spirit guides are more specific and look after one individual.

Guardian angels exist and there's nothing wrong with praying to them. While guardian angles can help you, it's best you focus on cultivating a relationship with your spirit guide instead.

Q. How many guides can a person have?

A. There are individuals who claim to have a spirit guide who stays with them throughout their lives. However, it's more likely their guardian angel. During your lifetime, you have at least one spirit guide. You can also have multiple guides.

Your spirit guides can also change as various guides can help with your different learning and developmental stages. Your relationship with your guide is a synergistic one.

This means that when you work with your spirit guide, you can create a better result than you would if you worked just by yourself. Thus, teamwork can get you stronger and better results.

Q. Are there male and female spirit guides?

A. Your spirit guide doesn't have a gender. However, some guides are inherently more feminine, or more masculine. If you have a lot of masculine energy, then your spirit guide will likely manifest masculine energy also.

Q. Can our spirit guides constantly see us?

A. Your spirit guides are always with you 24/7.

Spirit guides are not concerned with the physical realm. They don't sleep; they don't eat. They only care about your spiritual wellbeing.

You're here to learn things on the physical plane. However, you're also a spiritual being in a physical body. You're not a physical person with spiritual experiences.

Q. Can spirit guides move objects?

A. Although rare, there are instances wherein spirit guides have been observed moving things.

Q. Do spirit guides communicate only during meditation?

A. Meditation is not the only time your spirit guides can talk to you. They can talk to you at any place, any time, and anywhere. You just need to be aware of them through the five senses. At any time, guides can show you all kinds of messages and signs.

Meditation's purpose may be so that you can more easily connect with your guides and become more receptive of their messages. Meditation and prayer helps to open up the channel for your spirit guide to better communicate with you.

Spirit guides can talk to you at any time and they can communicate with you at even the most unlikely instances, say, during a meeting at work. When they talk, you'll experience and feel their presence, and then you know you need to act on something.

Thus, be aware and be open to any message that you may encounter at any time during the day, or even when you sleep.

Q. What is my spirit guide's name?

A. Your spirit guides are not particular with what you name them. There may be some guides who have a name which they reveal to you. Other guides will want you to call them by a name that you choose, much like parents naming their children.

Once you know your guide's name, or once you've given your guide a name, stick with it.

Q. Are there evil entities and guides?

A. The temporal realm is rife with evil energy. However, such evil beings can never be spirit guides. Spirit guides are good, and their light dispels the darkness always. When you allow yourself to be surrounded by white positive light, you're safe and evil can't touch you.

Never call on evil spirits by conjuring them. If you ask and pray for white light, it will dispel all darkness and evil from you. When you let yourself be surrounded by white light, evil cannot hurt you.

Q. Does it seem like your inner voice when spirit guides talk?

A. Yes, that's usually the case. However, you need to be open to the various ways your spirit guides can communicate with you. You may feel things, hear their voice, or sense things. Don't limit your guide to a specific way of delivering messages to you.

Q. How do I know I'm not making or imagining things up?

A. If you think your mind is just playing tricks on you, one thing you can do is test the answer. When your guides want to send you a message, they ring the doorbell. If you don't answer, they leave. They will often come back again and try to send the message multiple times.

However, there are messages that may seem unclear to you. Thus, it's imperative you keep an open mind. If you think you're imagining things, just ask your guides and test them.

For example, you wake up and have an overwhelming feeling that you need to quit your job. If you're confused as to who is sending this message, just ask your guides, "Do you want me to quit my job?" Your guides will then answer you, and they'll continue to send you messages. If you don't hear back from them, let the thought go.

Q. Can spirit guides help with communicating with departed loved ones?

A. Yes, spirit guides can help you connect with your deceased loved ones. The key to communicate with your loved ones who have passed on is to let your guides act as ambassadors.

Allow them to be the conduits between you and your loved ones. Letting them be ambassadors is a wonderful way to have an excellent relationship with your guides.

Q. I did something bad and feel guilty about it. Do you think my guide is communicating with me?

A. Yes, guilt is a powerful way for your spirit guides to have a conversation with you. Your conscience guides you. Your conscience is actually your spirit guide trying to communicate with you.

If you did wrong and you feel guilty about what you did, your spirit guides are telling you to correct your mistake. As soon as possible, fix the problem in order to have good karma. If you don't fix it soon, the guilt may only become stronger.

Your spirit guides aim to put you on the right spiritual path. They use feelings and emotions to convey their messages to you.

Conclusion

Thanks again for taking the time to read this book!

You should now have a good understanding of spirit guides, and how to communicate with them.

If you enjoyed this book, please take the time to leave me a review on Amazon. I appreciate your honest feedback, and it really helps me to continue producing high quality books.

www.ingramcontent.com/pod-product-compliance
Lightning Source LLC
LaVergne TN
LVHW020447080526
838202LV00055B/5373